jeans	T-shirt	sandals
leggings	shorts	slip
socks	shoes	boots	skirt
jeans jacket	sweatshirt
dress	fleece-shirt	cap
trainers	belt	pyjamas

head	shoulder	knee	toe
eye	ear	hand	nose	leg
arm	back	finger	neck
elbow	bottom	stomach
right hand	left hand

Miller * Green * Parker * Black * Collins

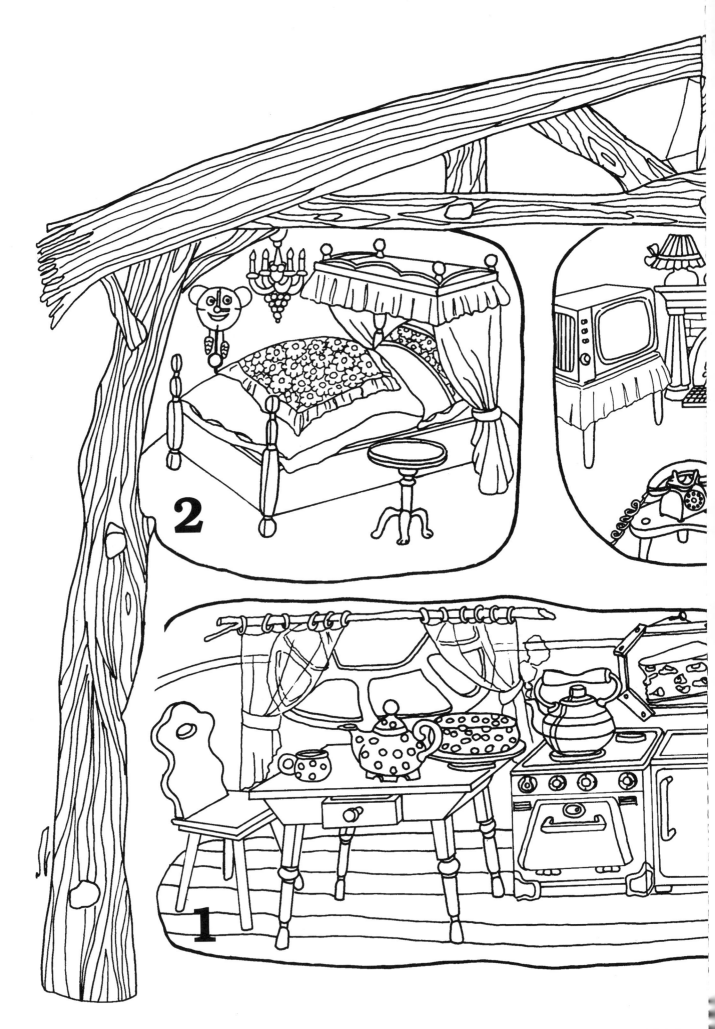

8

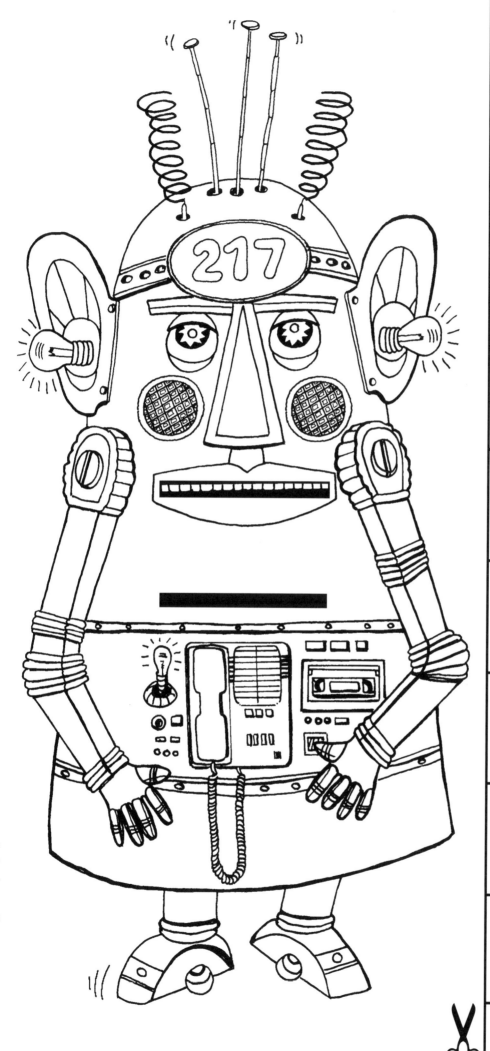

1	**Bring me your *bag*.**
2	**Go *six* steps.**
3	**Clap your hands.**
4	**Go to the *door*.**
5	**Open the *door*.**
6	**Come back.**
7	**Sing ...**
8	**Draw ...**
9	**Write ...**

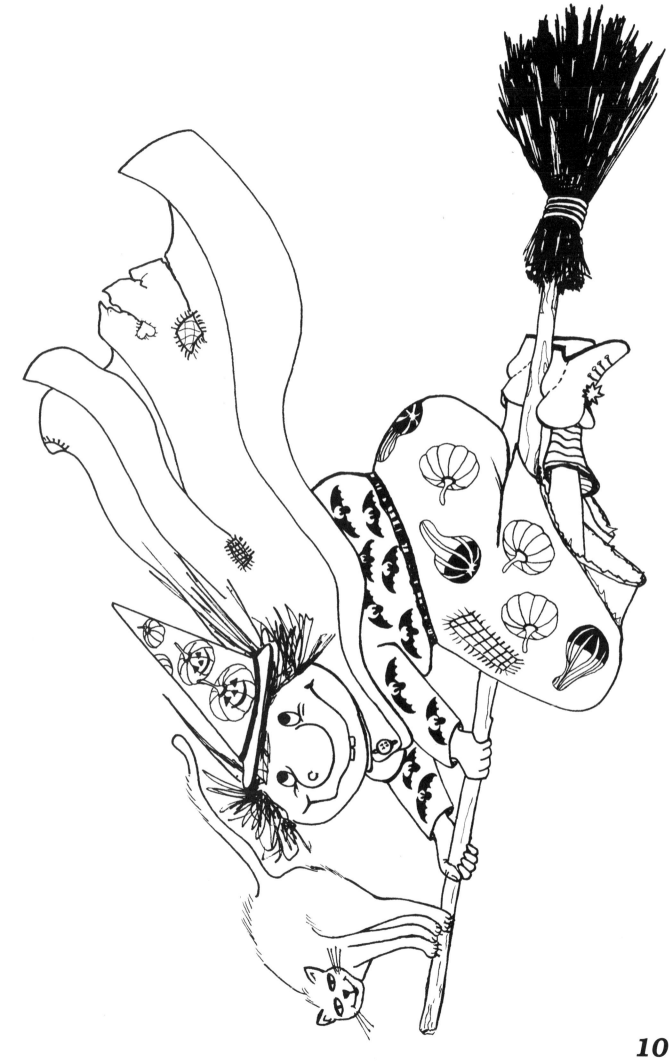

"I hear them"

I hear them, I hear them, I hear them on the roof!
The rein-deer are com-ing I hear them on the roof!
With a jin-gle, jin-gle bell and a clop, clop, clop,
and a clat-ter, clat-ter, clat-ter, on the chim-ney top;
I hear them, I hear them, I hear them on the roof!

What is it?

It's very cold and white.

It has got a ⊙ _____ and a black 🎩 _____.

It has got 2 black 👁 👁 _____ and a long red 👃 _____.

It has got a black ⚬⚬⚬ _____.

It has got a 🧹 _____ and 3 ⊙ ⊙ ⊙ _____.

It has got no 🦵🦵 _____ and no 👂👂 _____.

___

**mouth * hat * nose * legs * ears * buttons
eyes * broom * head**

14

My weather report:
Dublin * London * Dover * Plymouth

_____

_____

_____

_____

1	It's windy.
2	It's sunny.
3	It's rainy.
4	It's frosty.
5	It's cloudy.
6	It's foggy.
7	It's snowy.

Loch Ness
Aberdeen
Edinburgh
Londonderry
Dublin
Limerick
Manchester
Oxford
London
Bristol
Dover
Plymouth

15

①ear ③head ⑤neck ⑦arm ⑨bottom ⑪shoulder
②eye ④nose ⑥hand ⑧leg ⑩stomach ⑫elbow

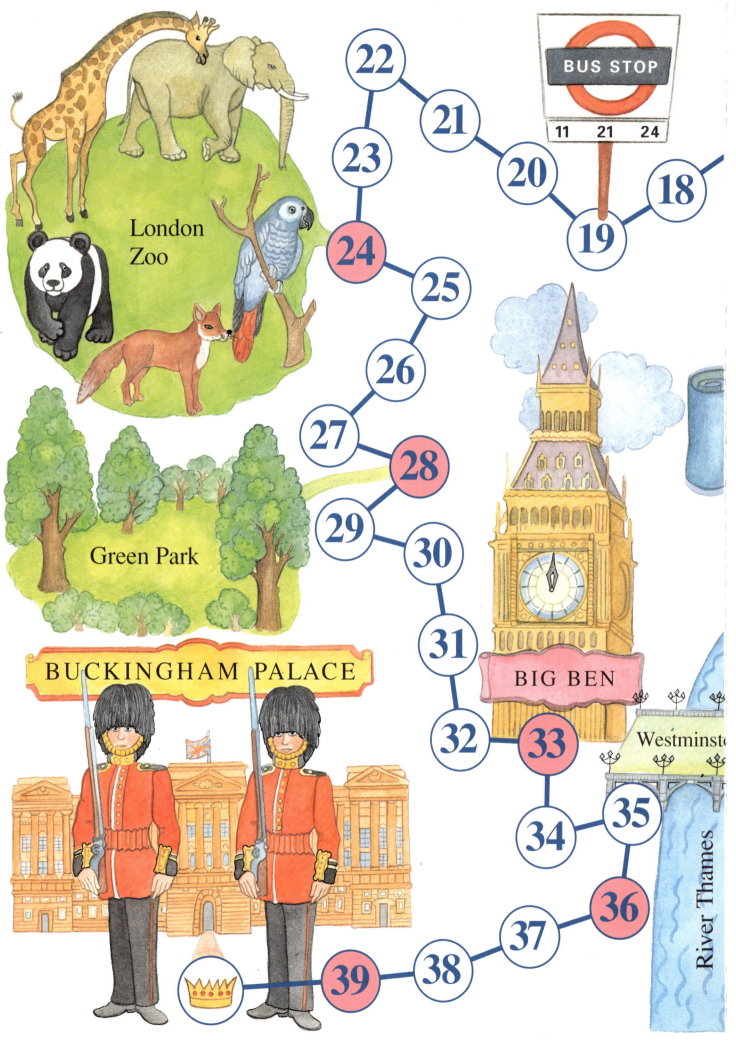

London

③ Here's your taxi.
   Go to number ten.

⑥ Tower Bridge is up.

⑦ Fine. Go to number 13.

⑫ You hot dogs.

⑲ Here's your bus.
   Go to number 23.

㉔ You go into London Zoo.

㉖ Go to number 29.

㉘ You love Green Park.

㉛ Go to Westminster Bridge. It's number 35.

㉝ Look – this is BIG BEN.
   It's 12 o'clock. Listen and

㉞ Good. Go to number 37.

㊱ Look at your picture cards of London.

㊴ Sorry! You must go back to number 30.

㊵ Great! Here's BUCKINGHAM PALACE.
   The 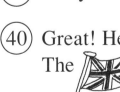 is up. Visit the Queen ...

* *End of the game* *

 Let's play

19

Stop juggling, Violet!   **Easter is coming.**

Scrambled eggs for dinner.

○ Oh no!
Look at the eggs!
CRACK! CRACK!
Violet is very sorry.
Mother Cottontail
has got a good idea.

○ Mother Cottontail
colours Easter eggs.
Violet wants to help.
She says,
"Can I help you, Mummy?"

○ Violet starts juggling.

○ Violet jumps onto the table
and starts juggling
with five white eggs.
Mother Cottontail says,
"Stop juggling, Violet!"

○ It's dinner time.
The Cottontail family has
scrambled eggs
for dinner.

○ The Cottontail family
colours Easter eggs.
Father Cottontail
mixes the colours.

○ Violet puts a white egg
into the hot water.

20

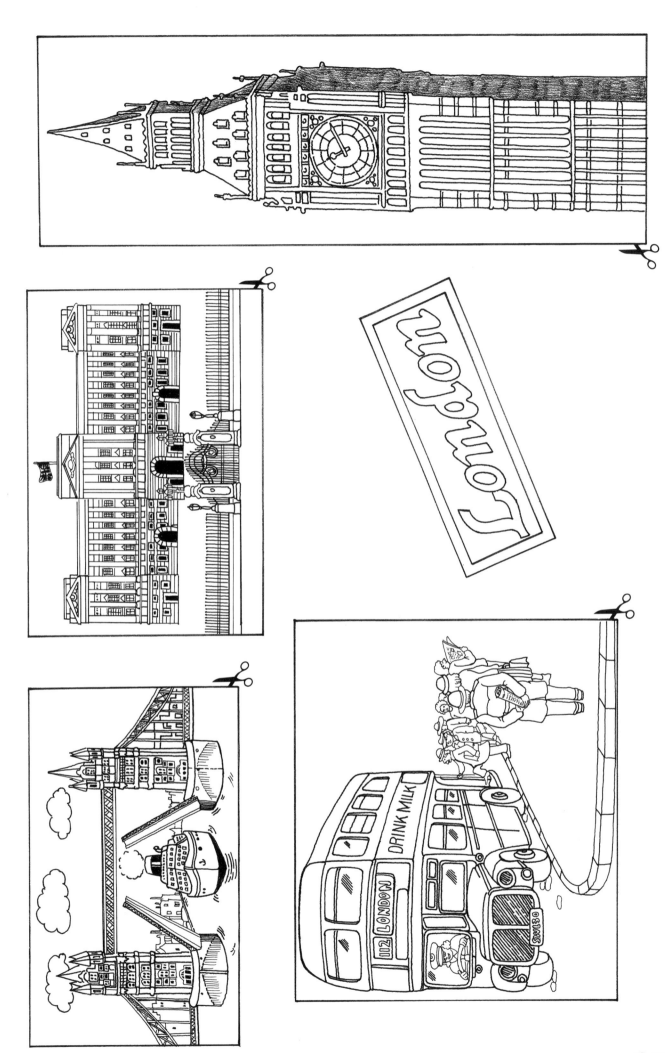

25

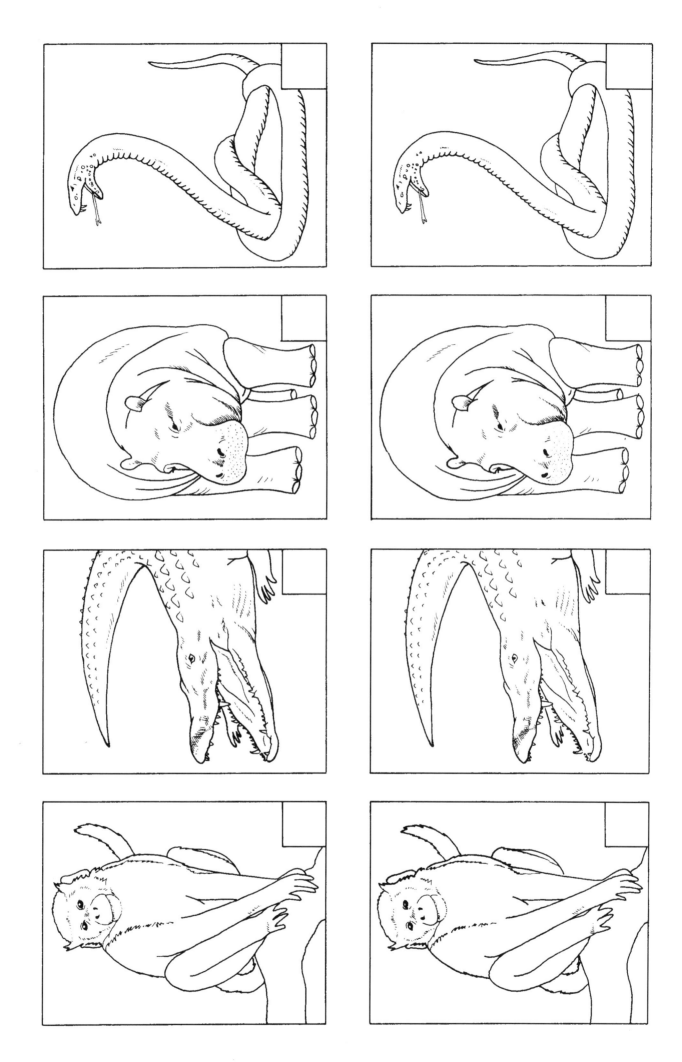

dog * cat * frog * spider * pig * wolf * panda * mouse * hen * fox * duck

Number 1 is a green . Number 2 is a pink . Number 3 is a blue .

Number 4 is a brown . The is number 5. It's orange.

The is number 6. It's green. The is number 7. It's black and pink.

The is number 8. It's violet. Number 9 is a yellow .

Number 10 is a little . It's white, yellow and red.

Number 11 is a red and green 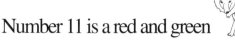.

29

The story of the three little pigs

Hink, Hank,	
and Oink:	We want to build a little house.
Mother:	All right. Be careful when you see the big bad wolf.
Hink, Hank,	
and Oink:	Don't worry, Mother. Goodbye.

Hink:	Can I have your straw, please?
Farmer 1:	Well - yes. Here you are.

Hink builds a little house of straw.

Wolf:	Hey, little pig! Open the door and let me in!
Hink:	No, no, no - you are the big bad wolf!
Wolf:	So I'll huff and I'll puff - and I'll blow your house down!

Hank:	Can I have your twigs, please?
Farmer 2:	Well - yes. Here you are.

Wolf:	Hey, little pig! Open the door and let me in!
Hank:	No, no, no - you are the big bad wolf!
Wolf:	So I'll huff and I'll puff - and I'll blow your house down!

Oink:	Can I have your bricks, please?
Farmer 3:	Well - yes. Here you are.

Wolf:	Hey, little pig! Open the door and let me in!
Oink:	No, no, no - you are the big bad wolf!
Wolf:	So I'll huff and I'll puff - and I'll blow your house down!

Wolf:	Little pig! Here I come!!!

The big bad wolf falls into the pot of hot water.

Hink, Hank	Goodbye, Mr Wolf.
and Oink:	I'm so happy to see you - so happy, so happy to see you.
	I'm so happy to see you - so happy to see you again.

31

name	drinks	☺	☹	😄
	milk			
	tea			
	cocoa			
	fizzy water			
	lemonade			
	coke			
	apple-juice			
	banana-juice			
	orange-juice			
	water			
	coffee			